THE COMPLETE BOOK OF

BIRDHOUSES AND FEEDERS

BY MONICA RUSSO & ROBERT DEWIRE

BONANZA BOOKS
New York

This 1989 edition is published by Bonanza
Books, distributed by Crown Publishers, Inc.,
225 Park Avenue South, New York, New York
10003, by arrangement with Sterling Publish-
ing Co., Inc.

Manufactured in the United States of America

Library of Congress Cataloging-in-Publication
Data

Russo, Monica.
    [Complete book of birdhouses & feeders]
    The complete book of birdhouses and
feeders/by Monica Russo and Robert
Dewire.
        p.   cm.
    Reprint. Originally published: The
complete book of birdhouses & feeders,
New York : Drake Publishers, 1976.
    Includes bibliographical references.
    ISBN 0-517-69314-3
    1. Birdhouses. 2. Bird feeders.
3. Birds—United States.
I. Dewire, Robert.   II. Title.
QL676.5.R87   1989
690'.89—dc20   89-18099
                                          CIP

ISBN 0-517-69314-3

h g f e d c b a

PREFACE

There are over 600 species of birds to be found within the continental United States. No matter where one goes, there will be birds to see. They are present all seasons of the year and there are many species that can be attracted, whether you own several acres of property or live in an apartment.

Attracting birds is fast becoming a major pastime in this country. In my job as a nature center naturalist I receive many inquiries on feeding and housing birds. This book is designed to answer those questions and to give you a start at enjoying the birds of your area.

In closing, I would like to gratefully acknowledge the able assistance of my wife Mary Jean whose critique and fine editing helped to complete the book.
Enjoy and use it.

R.C.D.

CONTENTS

THE BIRDS TO BUILD FOR

The following selection of birds are those which will accept bird boxes, platforms, or climbing vines on a home or trellis. Whether or not a bird chooses the home you set out may not follow the established guidelines. If the entrance hole is big enough, birds of many species will readily accept a house whether it was "designed" for them or not.

THE BLUEBIRDS

Bluebirds have long brought enjoyment to man — dating back to the Plymouth colony where the early settlers called them blue robins, as they reminded them of a blue version of the English robin so familiar to them. Three species of bluebirds are found across our country.

The eastern bluebird, ranging across the eastern two-thirds of the country, has a solid blue back, deep orange upper breast, and white lower breast. The western bluebird takes in the remaining third of the country and has a blue throat with the orange below it. The back

is blue with some orange across the upper part. Mountain bluebirds are also western; they have solid blue backs, and pale blue breasts, completely lacking any orange.

These birds readily accept bird boxes as nest sites, using old woodpecker cavities as natural sites where there are no boxes. The arrival of the starling and English sparrow, which also prefer tree holes, have caused a serious decline in the bluebird populations, especially the eastern species where the starling and sparrow first became established. With the spread of these two birds westward, the two western blue-birds are also beginning to have problems.

Bluebirds begin to nest very early in the spring, with nest sites selected and nest building underway in March and early April. Normally, five beautiful blue eggs are laid. Young are fledged by early summer and a second brood will often be started.

Bluebirds are members of the thrush family, and like their cousins the robin and the brown thrushes, are insect eaters during the spring and summer. In the fall, they often turn to berries for part of their diet, relishing such types as blueberry, cherries, and bayberry. Many bluebirds will remain in the northern half of the country all winter, subsisting on berries such as junipers and sumacs.

When hunting insects, bluebirds will sit on a fence post, shrub, or branch of a tree overlooking a field. All of a sudden the bluebird will fly to the ground snatching up an insect, then return to its perch to feed. I never tire of watching these birds feed: brilliant flashes of blue, flying to and from their perch. In the winter, flocks of ten or more may gather at stands of sumac or in fields of red cedar, the blue matching the sky on a clear day.

It is certainly worthwhile setting out a bluebird house or two, especially if you have seen a bluebird in your area. To have them established on your property can bring nothing but pleasure.

THE TREE SWALLOW

Tree swallows are the first of our native swallows to head north in the spring. Most reach the northern states by late March and early April. They are hardy birds, many of them remaining in the southern states through the winter while our other swallow species usually migrate out of the country. Water areas are the first place where the migrants congregate as they fly back and forth over the water's surface snapping up insects.

These are handsome swallows with pure white underparts and irridescent backs that appear green at one angle and blue at another. They are not colonial although they will tolerate others of their kind nesting within a dozen yards or so. If several nest boxes are put up in an area, the tree swallows will stage elaborate flights before choosing a nest site.

The birds race back and forth from one box to another, one or more birds sitting on a box or circling around it slowly and then heading off to another box. All the while, the birds are calling a series of notes that have a hurried quality to them that seems to go along with their hectic activity.

Once a site is chosen, nest building begins. The swallows use grasses primarily but have a particular affinity for adding feathers. If swallows are flying back and forth over an area and you have access to some feathers, from an old feather pillow perhaps, take some and throw them up in the air as the birds fly over. The swallows will pick them up, toss them around, and eventually take them to their nest box. Tree swallows are very tolerant of close approach. A bird will sit on top of the box or poke its head out of the hole, not flying until one is only a few feet away.

Once nesting is completed, the birds begin forming huge flocks for the migration south. They will sit so close together on telephone lines that the wire will not be visible for long stretches. In other areas, they will mass over shrubs or cover roads or rooftops. They seem to flock in the greatest numbers along coastal areas where numbers in the tens of thousands are not unusual. It is also a time when these swallows add an unusual item to their diet. Unlike the other swallow species which are strictly insect eaters, the tree swallows now eat berries in large quantities. They are mostly bayberry, a common shrub especially along the coast. This diet is beneficial to them since many do not head south until late fall when insects begin to get scarce

Tree swallows, common, easy to attract, and enjoyable to watch, are pleasant birds to have nesting on your property. A bluebird-size bird house and a small open area are the main requirements for success

THE HOUSE WREN

The house wren is a familiar and welcome addition to the backyard of any homeowner who sets out birdhouses. From the time the wrens arrive to establish territories in early spring until the conclusion of nesting in late summer, the energy of these tiny brown birds seems endless. The male begins singing soon after finding a suitable location, and the singing goes on through the raising of the young, long after other species of birds have stopped. The song is a delightful and bubbly mixture of notes surprisingly loud for so small a bird. From sunrise to sunset, even on the hottest of days, the wren sings from the nest site.

The presence of man has benefited the house wrens by providing more nest sites than were available in woodland areas. The wrens are tree-hole nesters, and finding natural nest sites such as

16

woodpecker holes was a highly competitive process with other birds.   The wren, being very tolerant of man, has gladly moved into his suburban areas utilizing such unusual nest sites as tin cans, mailboxes, and old boots. One nest was built on the rear axle of a car that was driven daily, the wrens traveling with it, and surprisingly, successfully raising their young! I have even seen a wren nest constructed in a pair of Bermuda shorts that were left hanging on a clothesline for several days!

Bird houses are the easiest way to attract wrens to your property. By making the entrance hole 1¼ inches in diameter it restricts the larger birds that might otherwise compete with the wren. This is not to say that a wren cannot hold its own against larger birds; in fact they are so persistent that they usually will win when challenged for a nest site.

Once a site is found the wrens will build their nest. They are primarily made of sticks, with some of such surprising length that it is a wonder how these birds can maneuver them through the small opening. The energetic bird will also proceed to fill other nearby bird boxes with sticks if they are not otherwise occupied.

The wrens become even more active when the young hatch. Watching the pair flying back and forth with food, the male taking time out to regularly

18

burst into song, can make you feel tired. Observations have shown the incredible activity of a male bird which fed young from 4:15 A.M. till 8:00 P.M. on a single day and made 1,217 visits to the nest with food!

To the average person, the wren is probably one of the most appealing of all birds. The ease of attracting it to even a small backyard, its pleasant song, and the fact that it consumes an enormous number of harmful insects combine to make this tiny bundle of energy with cocked tail a real favorite.

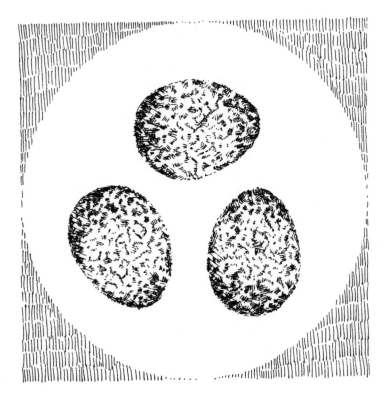

CHICKADEES & TITMICE

Chickadees and titmice are members of the same family, both types characterized by lively yet tame behavior, and they are favorites to almost everyone. They are best known as regular visitors to winter bird feeders to which they fly to pick out a choice seed and then dart off again to a nearby tree to pick it open and eat the contents. Many of the species can be fed from the hand if one has a little patience.

There are seven species of chickadees and four of the titmice. Of these, the black-capped chickadee of the northern states across the country, the Carolina chickadee of the southeast, the tufted titmouse of the eastern

half of the country, and the plain titmouse found in portions of the west, are the four most likely to make use of bird boxes.

These birds all use tree holes for natural nesting sites, either moving into an old one, or in many cases, pecking one out of a dead tree themselves. Choosing a bird house to nest in is somewhat of a chance thing. Anyone who has these birds established as winter residents at their feeders could possibly get them to nest.

With the arrival of spring, the whistles of these birds are heard everywhere. The titmice have a two-note "Peter, Peter" whistle, the black-capped chickadee a clear "fee bee" whistle, and the Carolina chickadee a four-note whistle, each note a different pitch. Nests are made of grasses, feathers, and often a quantity of the soft down found on the fiddleheads of the cinnamon and interrupted ferns that are poking through the ground at nest building time.

During nesting season, these birds will

change their diet almost completely to insect food which they feed to their young until they are nearly fledged. If one has a small feeder of sunflower seeds available in late summer, the adult birds will bring the young to the feeding area, leaving them on a branch. The adults will then take seeds, open them up, and proceed to feed the young — a most enjoyable sight to watch.

In the fall, family groups may band together in small flocks and roam the woods looking for food. Chickadees and titmice are very acrobatic, hanging upside-down, fluttering before an opening in a tree, and investigating every inch of a branch for a hidden mass of insect eggs or larvae to eat. Often, other migratory species such as warblers, kinglets, and woodpeckers will join them.

Watching these birds at feeders all winter long is fun, but they seem to disappear when summer comes. Having a bird box up might persuade them to stay.

THE FLICKERS

The common flicker is our one native woodpecker that readily accepts bird boxes to nest in. There are records of our other species of woodpeckers occasionally going into a bird house, but the flicker is the only one to regularly occupy them. This is not to say that they could not easily peck out a hole in a tree as other woodpeckers do, it is just that flickers seem to have a more varied taste for nest sites.

Originally thought to be three distinct species, the three flickers of the United States are now considered subspecies. Handsomely colored, all have a black bib, a pale breast spotted black, brown back and wings speckled black, and white rump. The eastern race (yellow-shafted) has a red stripe on the back of the head, a buffy face, gray crown, and gold under the wings and tail. The southwestern race (gilded), has the same gold below, but a brown crown, gray face, and no red on the back of the head. The western race, (red-shafted flicker), has red under the wings and tail, and head markings are the same as the gilded race. Males are separated from females by the presence of a "mustache" on the face, black on the yellow-shafted, and red on the gilded and red-shafted flickers.

Flickers are more often seen feeding on the ground than any of the other woodpeckers. This is due to one of the major food items in their diet — ants! Upon locating an ant hill, a flicker will simply snap up the ants as they come out, or dig into the hill with the long powerful bill in pursuit of the ants, using its long sticky tongue to catch them.

In the fall, flickers also eat a great deal of plant food; they especially favor the many varieties of berries including those of the poison ivy. While most leave the

northern United States in fall, some remain where berries are plentiful, and they may also eat suet at bird feeders where their aggressiveness will even keep the starlings away while they feed

   The call is a series of loud, sharp "flicker" notes which is often combined with the loud drumming on a hollow tree which can be heard for great distances. Both call and drumming are a welcome sign of spring throughout the northern parts of the country

THE AMERICAN KESTREL

When one thinks about attracting birds to his property, rarely does he consider a bird of prey as a possibility. The hawk to be considered here is the smallest of our hawks, the American kestrel. It is slightly smaller in size than our jays and is found throughout the United States. It is a bird of open areas and is often seen along roadsides perched on a power line, telephone pole, fence, or fence post. In flight, it displays the sleek, pointed wings characteristic of all the fast flying birds of the falcon family.

The kestrel is among the prettiest of our hawks. Males have red backs with black barring and blue-gray wings. The head is a bold pattern of black, white, and red; the tail is red, Tipped with black and white. The front is buff with fine dark speckling. Females lack the blue wings; rather, they are colored like the back, and the tail is barred with black its entire length.

Until recently, the kestrel was given the common name of "sparrow hawk". The connotation of this name indicated that birds were its primary diet. Actually, birds are rarely taken except in winter when other food is difficult to find. Normally, the kestrels feed on small rodents and in the summer will feed almost entirely on such insects as the large locusts and flying grasshoppers. The name change is thus a good one ∽

The hunting technique of the kestrel is fun to watch, the bird flying over a field and suddenly stopping and hovering in mid-air ten or more feet up. The bird will remain in a fixed position rapidly beating its wings waiting for the right moment to descend upon its prey; this hovering may last a minute or more. Suddenly, it will drop feet first to the ground soon to come up again with its prey. Flying to a post or other convenient spot, the kestrel will

feed at leisure ❧ ❧

Kestrels will nest in bird houses although they usually use tree holes. The flicker-sized box is the most commonly used. I know of one bird that had a nest at the corner of the porch of a house where there was an opening into the attic large enough for it to fit through. The kestrels returned there to nest for several years. The major requirement for having this bird around is satisfying its need for a large open area where it can find food easily. A house in the open on a high post might result in establishing this handsome falcon, one of the unusual birds people can attract ❧ ❧

Owls are birds rarely seen by the average person. Their nocturnal habits limit sightings to the chance discovery of a roosting bird in an evergreen grove or sitting at the entrance of a tree cavity. It is much more common that an owl is heard, with hardly a place in the country where at least one or more species cannot be heard on a spring night.

Of all the owls, only two will make use of bird houses. The small saw-whet owl of the northern border of our country is one, usually occupying a flicker box. Although it is a rarely encountered owl, it is extremely tame when found. Records abound of people who have been able to

33

reach up and pick one of these birds off a tree branch where it was roosting.

The more common owl to be found throughout the country is the screech owl. These owls will occupy either flicker or wood duck boxes and their presence will often go undetected as they confine their activity to night, although an adult bird may peer from the hole by day.

Screech owls are small, standing about eight inches high and having small tufts of feathers on the head resembling ears or horns. The birds have three color phases: gray, brown, and red. There seems to be no genetic determination in these colors as all three phases may show up in a single brood.

The screech owl does not "screech"; the call instead being a series of tremulous notes going down the scale or a whistled trill all on one pitch. Bird watchers have discovered that the owls will quickly respond to a tape recording of the call played at night. By day, the recording attracts numbers of songbirds seeking to "mob" the owl.

For the most part, these owls are rodent eaters although insects such as large moths and beetles are often consumed during the summer.

In addition to using boxes for nesting, both screech and saw-whet owls are quick to occupy a house left out in the winter as a roosting site. A quick way to determine if owls might be in your area is to listen for them calling, usually within an hour after sunset. If you hear one, a check of the box during the day may find a roosting bird in it which should not be disturbed. Screech owls are often found in suburban areas and it might be fun to put out a flicker box just to see if you can attract one of these little owls

THE WOOD DUCK

When it comes to birds of striking colors and patterns in the United States, few can rival the drake wood duck in breeding plumage. To describe the bird is just about impossible. The bold patterns of white and reds combine with areas of irridescence that change color as the angle of light varies. The "woodies", as they are commonly called, are found throughout the country during nesting season, moving to the southern areas when winter temperatures freeze their swamplands.

Wood ducks are denizens of woodland swamps and small wooded ponds and streams, often appearing in such areas within close range of homes. To the casual observer, the wood ducks seem

38

strange indeed. Instead of spending most of their time in the water or along the shoreline, these birds will fly up into the trees, perching like songbirds. They do not "quack" as one expects ducks to do. Males have a whistle that goes up the scale, while the harsh cries of the females, heard most often as they hurtle through the trees after being flushed, are reminiscent of the cries of an animal in distress. Add to this the fact that these ducks nest in holes in trees and you have a bird that seems to break most of the behavior patterns of ducks.

The males' coloration and the habit of nesting in tree cavities almost resulted in the extinction of this spectacular bird. At the turn of the twentieth century, the males were hunted relentlessly for taxidermy mounts and for their feathers which were used in tying fishing flies. At the same time, vast areas of swampland, deemed worthless at the time, were being destroyed resulting in the loss of nesting trees. The federal government stepped in and stopped all hunting in 1918 but nesting space remained a problem. Experiments showed that the wood ducks would accept artificial homes in the form of birdhouses similar to those for songbirds. State Fish and Game Commissions in a number of states initiated programs of setting out hundreds of boxes in suitable habitats and encouraged property owners to do the same. The result has been a remarkable comeback of the wood duck, and a bright note in wildlife management.

THE WOOD DUCK NESTING BOX

The wood duck box can be put up by anyone who lives reasonably close to a swamp area. Wood ducks will nest as much as a quarter of a mile from a water source. On land, the box should be placed ten or more feet high to discourage predators, but over water it can be considerably lower. Except for feathers plucked from their breast, wood ducks do not build a nest, so a few inches of wood shavings in the box is a good idea. The ground under the box should not be hard or rocky since the day the young hatch from their eggs, they climb up the side of the box, aided by sharp claws for this purpose, and jump from the hole to the ground. The mother will then lead them to the nearest water. I have watched a mother wood duck take her nine young across two busy roads and through the front and back lawns of two homes to get to a small swamp-land

THE PURPLE MARTIN

Purple martins must certainly rank as one of the most beneficial of all our birds. Their diet consists solely of insects, many of which are harmful to man. A major food item is the mosquito, and it is a known fact that those fortunate enough to have nesting martins nearby also have fewer mosquitoes bothering them.

The martin is one of our swallows; in fact, the largest member of the family. Males are completely dark purple in color, often appearing black but showing an irridescence of purple in the correct light. Females are duller in color on the upperparts and have pale underparts.

Martins nest in almost all parts of the country. By March, nesting has begun in the South, and advancing

migrants move north, with some birds stopping off in each area to begin nesting, finally reaching the northernmost sites by mid-May. Males arrive first and establish nest sites. Colonial by nature, they much prefer the multi-holed bird houses people put up. Before houses were available, tree holes and rock crevices were the usual nesting locations. There are records of Indians putting out hollow gourds to attract these birds. Once established, colonies will return to the same location each year. One colony is known to have returned before their house was put up and they were seen fluttering around at the exact location and height of where the house should have been.

The greatest danger martins face is a sudden cold spell or storm period that persists for several days. If this should result in insects being inactive, it can spell tragedy. Three or more days of this kind of weather can mean starvation, and if it does not destroy the colony it almost certainly eliminates any nesting success for that year.

The most insects are consumed when the young have hatched and must be fed. During this time, both parents of each nest in the colony fly over the fields and marshes, around backyards, and over treetops chasing down every insect they can find. Extremely agile, as are all the swallows, they are even successful in catching those insect masters of the skies, the dragonflies ～

Late summer finds the martins moving south as they are very early migrants. By November, most have left the country for South America. Each year however, the purple martins return, and contribute to our enjoyment in the watching of their aerial acrobatics and in the knowledge that there are fewer mosquitoes to slap because of them ～

THE BARN SWALLOW

The barn swallow is the most streamlined of our swallows. The long, swept-back wings and deeply forked tail contribute to this effect. It is also the most colorful swallow with its deep blue back, orange front, and deeper orange throat and forehead. The shorter tail feathers have white spots at the tips.

This is the swallow of farmlands, although they are found in many other locations as well. It is difficult to find a farm that does not have at least a few of these birds. The barns serve as their nest sites. The swallows build their nests primarily of mud which they gather from the edges of puddles, ponds, or streams,

46

and carry in their mouths to the site. The inside of the nest is often lined with feathers; in farm areas, usually chicken feathers

The swallows raise up to six young and spend the daylight hours darting across the fields and over bodies of water filling their mouths with insects to bring back for the young. The food includes mosquitoes, flies, and many other species of insects which may be considered harmful to man. When the young first leave the nest, the parents will feed them as they perch on a power line or fence

Barn swallows start south in September, travelling in small flocks or sometimes mixing in with the large masses of tree swallows also heading south. While many of the tree swallows will remain in the southern parts of this country, the barn swallows will continue to migrate all the way to South America

Suburban areas will usually have small populations of barn swallows. They are most often found where there is an open pond or

47

field area. In these locations away from their traditional barns, they will look to houses for nest sites. The birds can be induced to nest under the eaves of a house if a platform is provided on which they can set the nest. Just as often, they will find a location which suits them without one's help. A garage which has the door left open is an attractive nest site, as is a carport, or under the balcony of the second floor of a house

These swallows are quite tame, and many enjoyable hours can be spent watching their aerial acrobatics or observing the feeding of the young. Their pretty colors, hurried but pleasant twitterings, and effective control of insects, all add up to a bonus which one receives when he is fortunate enough to have these birds nesting around his home

THE ROBIN

Robins are generally considered to be the number one sign of spring in the northern half of the United States. This is despite the fact that many robins can be found wintering in the north. These winter robins are usually northern birds from Canada. The robins present through the summer have indeed gone south, and it is the arrival of these birds which heralds spring

The northern robins are actually quite scarce, usually staying near stands of berry-bearing plants such as sumacs, hawthorns, and

crab apples. The average person will rarely see one. When March arrives, so do the robins that will be with us through the fall. Suddenly a suburban lawn that had no birds the day before will have ten or twenty robins all across the yard. To anyone seeing this, the reason is simple — spring has arrived!

Watching the robins feed on the lawn is most intriguing. The bird will stand motionless for several seconds, with its head cocked to one side. Suddenly it pecks down hard and comes up with a large worm you could have sworn wasn't there.

Sometime during April the males begin to sing. Members of the thrush family, their song is typical of most of the family in that they produce a pretty song of chips and whistles put together as a series of short melodies.

Robins are quite tolerant of man's presence, and getting them to nest on one's property is not difficult. They do not use

bird houses, but will accept a platform under the eave of a house, on which it can build its nest. Another favorite location is in evergreens, and houses with plantings of yews and arborvitaes along the front will often have robins taking up residence in them.

Nests are made of mud lined with grasses. The beautiful blue eggs are laid early in spring and a second brood will often be started in mid-summer. Young robins will be everywhere in summer, easily recognized by their pale orange breast speckled with black

By early fall, the evening skies are dotted with flocks of robins as they start south. Come spring, they return again to brighten the countryside with their song.

PHOEBES

Phoebes are among the earliest of all the insect eaters to return to the northern half of the country in the spring. The phoebes arrive by early April in most areas. John James Audubon conducted one of the first bird banding experiments on a family of phoebes when he tied some silver wire to the leg of some nesting birds and the following year observed at least two birds back in the area

Phoebes are members of the flycatcher family and three species are found in this country. The black phoebe of the southwest is dark gray except for a white belly. Say's phoebe is found throughout the west. Its head and back are brown; the tail is black. The belly is pale orange. Eastern phoebes are found in the eastern two-thirds of the United States; they are dark gray with a pale breast.

One characteristic of all phoebes is a tail-wagging behavior most evident just after a bird has landed on a perch. The tail will move up and down slowly several times and then stop.

When hunting for food, phoebes will sit and wait for an insect to pass by. At the right moment, the bird will dart out catching the insect with a loud snap of its bill that is audible at quite a distance. The early arrival of these birds can be disastrous if winter weather returns in April and insect food disappears.

Phoebes originally nested on rock outcrops but structures built by man have now provided many more locations which the birds readily accept. A favorite spot is

under bridges. Small bridges along country roads and New England's covered bridges will very often have a phoebe sitting on them, a sure sign that it is nesting under there. The bird will also move into barns and nest under eaves of houses, especially if a platform is provided. Carports are also a favorite location.

Nests of the eastern species are constructed of mud and moss while Say's phoebe uses a mixture of fine grasses to line the mud nest. Black phoebes add horse hairs to their mud nests.

The name phoebe is derived from the call of the eastern species, a harsh "spoken" call of "fee bee". The black-capped chickadee and mountain chickadee whistle a clear "fee bee" which many people mistake for a phoebe. Hearing the phoebes' call in April is always a welcome sign of spring.

THE HOUSE FINCH

The house finch has always been a common bird of the west. Also called linnets, they thrive in and around towns and cities, completely in harmony with man. Males are a bold red on the head, breast and rump; the wings, back and tail are brown. The lower breast is white, streaked with brown, a good field mark when distinguishing this bird from the similarly colored purple and Cassin's finches, both of which have unstreaked lower breasts. The female house finch is completely brown with a heavily streaked breast.

House finches will nest on or next to one's house if it has thick plantings around it. Vines on the side of a house are favorite spots.

Ivies, roses, and Virginia creeper are wall climbers that the birds will set their nests in. I knew some people who made the surprising discovery of a house finch nest set in the middle of a large fuschia which had been hung out on their porch for the summer.

The eastern part of the United States is now enjoying the establishment of these birds, thanks to a strange series of events that began in 1940. At that time, house finches were being illegally sold in New York City pet stores under the name "Hollywood finches". When the pet shop owners discovered they could be prosecuted under the Migratory Bird Treaty Act, the finches were released in large numbers throughout the New York City area. The birds adapted readily, and, in 1942, the first nest was discovered on Long Island. By 1958, they were established on western Long Island and in southwestern Connecticut. From here the spread continued, and the birds are now found from New Hampshire to Virginia with numbers increasing each year.

House finches are establishing themselves without disruption of species already present, mainly because they more closely associate with man than other birds care to. In winter, large flocks may mass at bird feeders, keeping other species away, often to the disappointment of the birdwatcher. The finches wander, though, and do not remain all day at a feeder, giving other birds a chance to feed.

By early spring, the bright warbling song of the male can be heard along suburban roadsides. Unlike other birds discussed in this section, one is less likely to attract house finches by setting out a bird house or platform, but if you have a thick hedge around your home or other favorable plantings, you may find this welcome bird already established on your property.

THE STARLING

The European starling is perhaps the most abundant bird in this country. Considering that the bird was non-existant here prior to 1890, it demonstrates a remarkable growth rate and adaptability. It all began when Eugene Scheifflin released 60 birds in Central Park, New York City in 1890, and 40 more one year later. He belonged to an active group of Shakespeare lovers who planned to introduce every species of bird mentioned in the master's works. The starlings' wide range of food choices, hardiness, and aggressive behavior allowed them to spread across the country so that flocks numbering hundreds of thousands may now be found

Viewing a single starling close up reveals a rather handsome bird. The black body is irridescent in the proper light as shiny purple or green. In spring and summer, the bill is bright yellow; in winter, the bill is dark and the body is heavily speckled with white. These are stocky-looking birds with short tails.

Starlings are unpopular with many people because of their aggressive behavior. They will completely dominate a bird feeder, especially if suet is present, and will remain as long as food is available, keeping other species away. In spring, they are an even more serious threat. They are tree hole nesters and their aggressive behavior resulted in their driving away native species such as bluebirds and tree swallows. As their numbers grew, the need for nest sites did too, and the result was a serious drop in populations of our native species, especially bluebirds. Bluebird nest box projects have somewhat controlled the starlings' effect on the bluebirds since the larger birds cannot fit into the

64

one and one-half inch diameter hole recommended for bluebird boxes.

There is a beneficial side to these birds as well. They are major destroyers of many harmful insects. In spring and summer, their diet is comprised mainly of these destructive insects, and include many species of caterpillars, beetles and weevils.

Starlings mass in large flocks in the fall, a mixture of adults and the all grey juveniles. Flocks will roost in woodlands and in city areas under bridges and overpasses. I have watched a steady stream of starlings flying to a roost under a bridge in Connecticut. The birds came steadily for almost an hour and there were easily 20,000 birds at this roost with others still coming in when it was too dark to see well.

Here is one bird that you don't have to do anything in particular to attract — it is probably already there.

THE ENGLISH SPARROW

The English sparrow, like the starling, was brought over from England and rapidly gained a foothold in this country. In the case of the sparrow, it was more like several footholds since during the period from 1850 to 1881 birds had been released and were establishing colonies in New York, in Portland, Maine; Galveston, Texas; Cleveland, Ohio; Iowa City, Iowa, and several other locations. The bird readily took to man's dwellings and had no trouble finding nest sites under eaves of buildings, in barns, and under porch roofs.

Also called house sparrow, the English sparrow is not a true sparrow. Instead it is a member of a family of birds called weaver finches of which there are no native representatives in the United States. Males are quickly recognized by the black throat and upper breast. In addition, they have a gray cap and rusty stripe behind the eye. Wings and back are brown, the lower breast gray. Females are dull colored, lacking the black, and identified from our native sparrows by the combination of a pale unstreaked breast and buffy stripe over the eye.

English sparrows travel in flocks much of the time and even tolerate others of their kind nesting only a foot or two away. The birds are somewhat noisy, their large flocks filling the air with loud chirping.

These are truly birds of the city. As you move to the suburbs, they are still present, but in fewer numbers. In the country, they may still be found in smaller numbers around farms, staying near barns, chicken coops, and the farm houses. It is in the large dense forests that the sparrows are rarely found.

This is the bird which poses the most serious threat to other bird box nesters, especially the bluebird, tree swallow, and purple martin. The sparrows are more aggressive than any of these and as such will drive away the other birds. Being the same size as the bluebird and swallow, one cannot reduce the entrance hole size to exclude them, as is done with the starling. In most areas where English sparrows are abundant, there are no nesting bluebirds.

The sparrow builds a large nest using a mixture of grass, sticks, feathers, paper, string, and almost anything else it can find. Two broods may be raised over the summer. During the nesting period, adults feed insects to the young, and this diet includes the harmful Japanese beetle.

Both the English sparrow and starling are striking examples of the affect that the arrival of a new species can have on native ones. It is a point to be considered whenever an attempt is made to introduce exotic animals.

FEEDING BIRDS

Since the type of feeder, food variety, and methods of feeding could fill a book twice this size, we have selected what we feel would work best. One should not limit himself, but experiment with ways to attract birds. What works well in one area may not be sucessful in another, and vice-versa. We do hope this will start you in the right direction.

FOOD SOURCES

There is a great variety of food available to put out at a feeding station. The only limit to the variety of items one can use is governed by the amount of money you wish to spend on bird food

It is possible to attract just about any bird that usually visits a feeding station by using only a few items. The following three seem to satisfy most species, and are nutrition- ally good for them as well.

1. Sunflower Seed: This will be eaten by just about every bird that comes to feeders. It is high in protein value

2. Mixed Seed or Wild Bird Seed: This is a mixture of several types of seeds that will vary depending upon the brand. The most common ingredients are red and white millets, peanut hearts, cracked corn, and sunflower seeds. This mixture is eaten by sparrows and

finches, but (except for the sunflower seeds), will not be taken by the chickadees, titmice, and nuthatches. These birds open seeds by holding them in their feet and pecking them open. The other seeds in the mixture are too small for them to open this way and thus are not used. By weight, the mixed seed is about half the price of sunflower seeds.

3. Suet: This is beef fat usually obtainable in sizeable chunks from any super-market. It is very inexpensive, and you may often be able to obtain pieces free from a local butcher. It is the substitute for insects which attracts woodpeckers and other insect eaters such as Carolina wrens, brown creepers, and mockingbirds.

In addition to the above, there are a few other foods worth considering.

1. Thistle Seed: Relatively new on the market, this is a real favorite with gold-finches, house and purple finches, pine siskins,

and redpolls. The tiny black seeds are imported from Ethiopia. The species of thistle grown there will not germinate in our climate, thereby preventing us from having to eradicate small prickly thistles from our yards each spring. It is the most expensive of the seeds, by weight being almost double the price of sunflower seeds.

2. Cracked Corn: Popular with cardinals, blackbirds, gamebirds, and waterfowl, it would not be necessary in a small backyard. It should be considered by larger property owners especially if ducks, pheasant or quail are wintering in the area.

3. Peanut Butter: This is expensive, but popular with many birds including most of the suet eaters. It is best put out mixed with suet, since there are records of birds choking on it.

4. Bread: Popular, but of poor nutritional value. It fills a bird up rapidly but is metabolized in a short time. Because of this, it is best to put bread out only in the morning. If a

bird eats bread in the evening, a cold night will find the bird without the energy to maintain body temperature until daylight. ∽

Added to the previous foods can be pieces of citrus, whole peanuts, berries, popcorn, raisins, and many other items. The decision of what to feed is up to the individual. Whatever one uses, hours of pleasure can be had watching an active feeding station ∽

FROM THE GROUND UP

If one decides to establish a feeding station on his property, it should be recognized that even before any feeders are put out, there is a major feeding area already present - the ground. There are many birds that prefer to feed on the ground and only go to a feeder erected above ground level when forced to. Not feeding on the ground may result in fewer species of birds present at your feeding station. Birds that prefer the ground include various sparrows, juncos, towhees, cardinals, and doves.

Feed should be scattered over a fairly large area, to allow a sizeable number of birds to feed at once. Ideally, there should be some cover nearby. A row of bushes, a brushpile erected for the winter by the feeder, even several discarded Christmas trees are quite satisfactory. All serve as protection from possible predators, be it a neighborhood cat or an enterprising sharp-shinned hawk attracted by the flocks.

The best seed to use on the ground is the mixed seed. The various millets and other scratch grain found in the mix are all favorites of the above mentioned birds. Putting straight sunflower seed here is usually a waste since squirrels will get most of it. Cracked corn should be included, especially if you have quail or pheasant coming regularly. The corn may also attract large numbers of blackbirds, grackles, and crows which may not be so desirable

Periodically, the feeding area should be raked up and the material discarded. Concentrations of birds both on the ground and at feeders above can create an unhealthy situation in the feeding area that could prove fatal to some birds

The ground is thus the place to start when beginning a feeding station. All you need is some mixed seed and you're ready to go!

HANGING FEEDERS

When one decides to put up a hanging feeder, the question immediately arises as to what kind of feeder to choose. To be confronted with the bewildering array of feeders available both commercially and home-made often confuses the issue even more. Here are a few suggestions concerning these feeders.

Hanging feeders are for those birds which prefer to feed off the ground. They are usually small in size and ideally designed for birds that come to the perch, take a seed, and fly off to eat it. This is the way chickadees, titmice, and nuthatches feed. Circular feeders allow birds to take seeds from all around the edge while the cylindrical types have several openings along the tube. Box-type feeders have trays into which seed spills from a

78

central reservoir. ⌾∽

These feeders should be filled exclusively with sunflower seed. The birds which eat them prefer this seed over all others, and if a mixed seed is used, will simply pick out the sunflower seed, leaving the rest uneaten.

Feeders are best hung with wire. String will rot in time, or more likely, will be chewed through by squirrells which then feast on the seeds spilled by the fallen feeder. Many of these small feeders are designed to be attached to a pole.

One should then choose a feeder according to the types of birds he wants to attract. If you have a platform feeder and are also using the ground area, then you are satisfying the needs of all seed eaters except chickadees, titmice, and nut-hatches. A hanging feeder should then be chosen to allow them constant access to sunflower seed. The cylindrical feeders can be restricted to chickadees and titmice almost exclusively by removing the perches. Birds can then get a seed only by hovering at an opening to pull it out. ⌾∽

SUET FEEDERS

In the colder areas of the United States, suet is a very desirable winter food source for the birds. Woodpeckers feed almost exclusively on it, and other birds including chickadees, jays, nuthatches and titmice will also take it from time to time. Unfortunately, it is also a favorite of starlings; once they discover a suet feeder they may dominate it much of the time and only the larger woodpeckers such as the flickers and red-bellied woodpeckers will be able to dislodge them

There are several ways to put out suet, the most important factor being to keep it out of reach of the many mammals that are also fond of it. Placing it up high will discourage dogs and cats, and hanging it from a long wire will make it difficult for raccoons and opossums to reach

The material used to enclose the suet is usually a plastic, cord, or metal screen mesh. It allows birds to simultaneously hang on with their feet, and poke their bills through the mesh to get chunks of suet. The only disadvantage to the plastic or cord mesh feeders is that they will be quickly destroyed if a squirrel is able to get to them. The metal feeders prevent squirrels from getting much of the suet. If metal screening is used, one-half inch mesh or larger is best so that the birds can easily get their bills through the screening.

Another type of suet feeder is made by taking a section of log and drilling holes at least 1½" in diameter along its length in several locations. Stuff the holes with suet and hang it up. This more natural-looking feeder works well, its one drawback being that it is usually emptied quickly. Since filling this every day may not be convenient, it is best to use this feeder in addition to a mesh feeder so that suet is always available

PLATFORM FEEDERS

These are feeders that are designed to attract birds which like to feed in flocks, and at the same time be off the ground. The feeders may either be set up on posts in a yard or attached to the house as window-shelf feeders

The platform feeder is the easiest to construct. Using one-half inch outdoor plywood, cut the size platform you want and treat it with wood preservative. Put a piece of molding along the edge to prevent the wind from blowing off the seed. At this point your feeder is complete and the final step is to attach it to a post in a convenient location. Either an old tree log or section of 4 x 4 will do well. Another good location for a platform is attached to a porch railing. Painted the color of the building, it looks attractive, and brings the birds up close for viewing.

Window-shelf feeders are available commercially. The best design is one that has a holder for suet at one end and a seed container at the other end that dispenses seed onto the tray from the bottom. These feeders probably provide the most enjoyment of all, allowing one to observe birds from inches away. Such field marks as the black line dividing the red on the male hairy woodpecker's head, and the two-tone bill of the tree sparrow (a black upper mandible and a yellow lower one), are often missed unless viewed closely.

These feeders should have mixed seed put on them. It is also a good idea to provide extra sunflower seed as well. If you are using thistle seed, this is the best location to put it as these feeders are the favorites of goldfinches, siskins, and house finches

On snowy days ground-feeding birds move up onto the platforms, so that a three-feet square platform might have thirty or more birds on it.

Above: On a platform feeder are two evening
grosbeaks (yellow and black with white wing
patches) and a goldfinch. They are found
throughout most of the country.
Opposite: Ground feeders of the western states.
Perched on a bramble is a Towhee (also called
a chewink); To the left, an Oregon junco, and
below, the head of a Steller's jay. Standing at
the right is a white-crowned sparrow

Opposite:
Eastern birds at hanging feeders: In the fore-
ground on a coconut-feeder are a tufted titmouse
with a white-breasted nuthatch waiting his turn.
In the background, on a homemade suet-log
feeder: left, is a red-bellied woodpecker (top of
head and the back of the neck are red) and on
the right a downy woodpecker. ᏈᏊ
On the commercial cylindrical feeder at the
right: on top, a purple finch (dark red with
white unstreaked belly; females are brown and
streaked below.) On the bottom is a pine siskin —
brown and streaked, and with yellow wing patches.

HUMMINGBIRDS

Hummingbirds are truly the jewels of the bird world. These brightly colored flashes of irridescence are a delight to watch as they dart from flower to flower. Their wings move so fast they appear as a blur. They are the only bird that can fly backwards

The western half of the United States has a virtual monopoly on these tiny birds, with seven species in the far west, and five more in the southwest. The east, on the other hand, has only one species — the ruby-throated hummingbird

Since these birds are mostly nectar feeders, the average feeding station will not attract them. This can easily be remedied by making a hummingbird feeder. Take a small plastic or glass vial, and at the open end

attach a piece of red vinyl or plastic cut in the shape of a flower. Fasten a wire around the vial at this end for hanging, and your feeder is complete. For the food formula, mix sugar in water at a ratio of two parts water to one part sugar. The most important thing to remember is to change the mixture fairly often as it will ferment in warm weather. The feeder is most effective when hung near a flower bed.

Flowers themselves are the best method of attracting hummingbirds. They greatly prefer red flowers so that such plants as trumpet-vines, weigelia, trumpet honeysuckle, flowering quince, and red-colored flowers of such species as salvia, gladiolus, petunias, and azaleas are among the favorites. In springtime, apple blossoms are often visited.

Hummingbirds are most often seen during the migrations. But whenever seen, they are among the most enjoyable birds to watch.

SQUIRREL PROBLEMS

One of the biggest problems that people have at their feeders is squirrels. These mammals will visit feeders in search of their favorite food, sunflower seed, and they will also eat other seed found in the mix, along with suet. It is their great love for sunflower seed, however, that makes them so unpopular at feeding stations. They will attempt to reach any feeder in which these seeds are placed. Their agility and daring will find them going to great extremes, and they are usually sucessful. Once a feeder is reached, it is quickly emptied and the birds are left with very little. Here are some suggestions to keep squirrels off your platform and hanging feeders.

The first thing one must do is to see that platform feeders are placed out in the open, away from tree branches from which squirrels can jump to the feeder. Hanging feeders should be hung near the end of a branch and away from other branches so that the only way a squirrel can reach a feeder is from above it.

The next step is to obtain some sheet aluminum at least fourteen to twenty inches wide. Most hardware and lumber stores sell it. You need a piece as long as it is wide for each hanging or post feeder, and a piece half the length of the distance around your platform feeder.

Cut the corners of the piece for your hanging feeder so that you have a circle. Puncture the center and slide it down the wire so that it rests just above the feeder. Squirrels will not be able to get over this baffle. On post feeders, set the aluminum circle just under the feeder. The squirrel can climb the post but cannot get around the baffle.

For platform feeders, cut the aluminum down the middle so that you have two strips seven to ten inches wide, that will wrap around the feeder. Attach the strips like an apron along the lower edge of the feeder using nails. The squirrels will not be able to get around the apron to reach the feeder. Their only possible recourse will be to jump from the ground, and this can be prevented by making certain that the feeder is at least five feet high.

You will always have squirrels at your feeding station, but at least these simple preventive measures will restrict their activity so that there will be food for all.

WATERWORDS

    Having water available at a bird feeding station is especially important during the winter months. Depending upon the closeness of open water, birds may travel quite a distance, perhaps a mile or two, to find an adequate source. A typical birdbath is sufficient at a feeding station. Keeping it from freezing over in winter is difficult, the addition of hot water being the easiest method. Birds seem to really enjoy the "warm bath" and will quickly get into the steaming water. ∽∾∾

    Aquarium heaters placed in the bath will keep the water open. Their installation involves having an outdoor electrical outlet and underground electrical cord put in. A birdbath must be at least six to eight inches deep to immerse the heater in; bricks or flat stones are then need-ed to build up the bottom so that the water is not more than two inches deep.

In summer, and in the warmer parts of the country, one of the best methods of attracting birds is by using a water drip bath. This is made by taking a bucket or other container and hanging it over the birdbath at a height of two to three feet. A very small hole in the bottom of the container will allow it to drip slowly into the birdbath. This dripping action has an extraordinary effect on birds and will attract many of our insect eaters that might otherwise not be seen at a birdbath. These include our woodland warblers, flycatchers, tanagers, and kinglets.

Even if water is nearby as a natural source, it is worth having a birdbath in your yard. It will be used by many birds and provide still another way to attract birds to your property.

QUESTIONS

Q: Should food be put out during summer?
A: You will find that there is little activity at feeders in early summer since adult birds spend most of their time catching insects to feed their young. I keep one hanging feeder filled with sunflower seed but put out nothing else. Suet spoils quickly in the heat, and interest in the mixed seed is almost non-existant. In late summer, I find myself rewarded when the adult cardinals, chickadees, and titmice bring their fledged young to the feeding station and line them up on a branch to be fed ∽

Q: Should I try feeding birds if I have a cat or if my neighbor does?
A: If you have a location where you can set up feeders in the open with no cover nearby for a cat to sneak up in, then the birds should not have any problems. If a cat does catch a bird, it is usually an old or weak bird. The

other alternative is to feed only from hanging feeders that are high out of the cats' reach. If
you own the cat, keep it inside during the early
morning when birds feed most heavily and take
it in again in late afternoon. Mid-day feeder
activity is slower so there is less chance that the
cat will pose a real problem. If it is a neighbor's
cat, you might ask him to do the same

D: Will the birds be in trouble if I go
away for a week or more in mid-winter and
feeding stops?
A: This is best answered based on where you
live. If there are other houses close by which have
some feeding stations, the birds will not have
any problems. The birds that come to your
feeders also visit all the others during the
course of the day. If you are in the country
with no neighbors or only a few who do not
feed, then there could be a problem as your
feeder is what the birds depend on. It is wise
to get a friend to stop by each day and

fill the feeders for you.

Q: Should I put out grit for the birds?
A: All birds need grit or small stones in their gizzards to help them digest their food. Birds usually can find it, and in winter there is a ready supply along sanded roads. If you do have some, there is no reason not to put it out, however. It is sufficient just to scatter it on the ground or on a platform feeder. ⌇

Q: Should I use metal perches?
A: There are records of birds which have had wet parts of their body touch metal parts of a feeder on a cold day and get stuck to it. These records are very rare however, and should not stop one from using feeders with metal parts. ⌇

Q: Is there any way to keep birds I do not want from coming to the feeder?
A: Depending upon the individual, different people consider different birds as "undesirable." Among those frequently included in this

list are starlings, English sparrows, jays, and pigeons. There is no really effective way to totally eliminate them. Starlings are controlled to some degree if you stop feeding suet which is their favorite food. This unfortunately also results in losing one's woodpeckers. Bigger birds can be kept out of some feeders by making openings too small for all but the little birds, but this may also keep out the large "desirables" such as evening grosbeaks. It usually ends up being a case of taking the bad with the good.

Q: How does one prevent birds from striking a large window?

A: Birds will sometimes injure or kill themselves by flying into windows, especially large picture windows, where they see a reflection of the outside, and think the woods are where the glass is. Very sheer curtains drawn across the window is effective, or one can tape strips of aluminum foil to the windows at one end, letting them blow freely. The combination of the moving foil and its reflecting light often keeps the birds away. ∽

Q: Will squirrels catch birds?
A: There are isolated records of squirrels suddenly grabbing a bird at a feeder and carrying it off. These incidents are rare and one should not worry about it.

Q: What can I do if a hawk is harassing my feeders?
A: Whenever birds are concentrated, as at a feeder, it is an invitation to any predator to take advantage. The sharp-shinned hawk is the species most often involved in this situation. It is usually scared off easily and this may be all that is needed to send it away. If the hawk persists, the best thing to do is restrict feeding to areas under bushes; a temporary brush pile may be put up with seed thrown inside it. The birds can feed safely, and the hawk usually moves on

BIRDSCAPING

Here is a selection of plants that are among the most attractive to birds. Many species that feed on the various fruits offered by these plants will not come to seed feeders, so these plants can increase the variety of birds that will come to your property. Checking with your local agriculture office or soil conservation service will enable you to find out which plants grow best in your area.

THE DOGWOODS

There are many species of dogwood found across the country. They vary in size from shrubs to trees reaching forty feet in height. Most species have clusters of tiny white flowers, but the flowering dogwood (called Pacific dogwood in the west) have large showy bracts around each flower cluster, giving the appearance of one large flower. The fruit of all the dogwoods are popular with birds, but the flowering dogwood berries seem to be the favorite. Bright red in color, they ripen in the fall and are quickly eaten by robins, waxwings, starlings, and thrushes. By winter, there are none left.

This is perhaps the most popular of all plantings for birds. In spring it is a handsome tree with its showy flower mass; in fall the leaves turn dark red. By late fall, next year's flower buds will be formed on the branches.

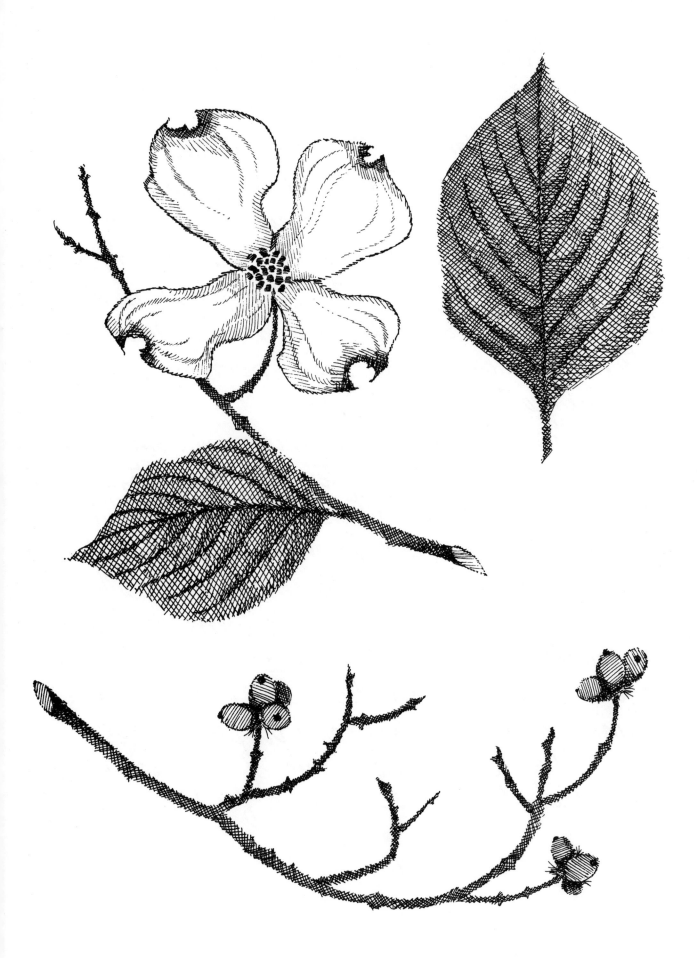

MULTIFLORA ROSE

A popular plant in recent years, the multiflora rose is often used as a border around property. It grows densely and its prickly stems are an effective barrier against predators. Because of this, the plant is a favorite nesting site of many birds including catbirds, yellowthroats, song sparrows, and yellow-breasted chats.

This plant flowers in June with small white flowers, yellow at the center. A large stand of these will display an attractive mass of white, and a delightful rose fragrance. The small rose hips are formed in late summer, and will serve as a food supply for the birds through the winter. Among the species I have seen regularly feeding on them are mockingbirds, robins, cedar waxwings, and purple finches.

The winter cover value of this rose makes it an ideal plant to set near a feeding station.

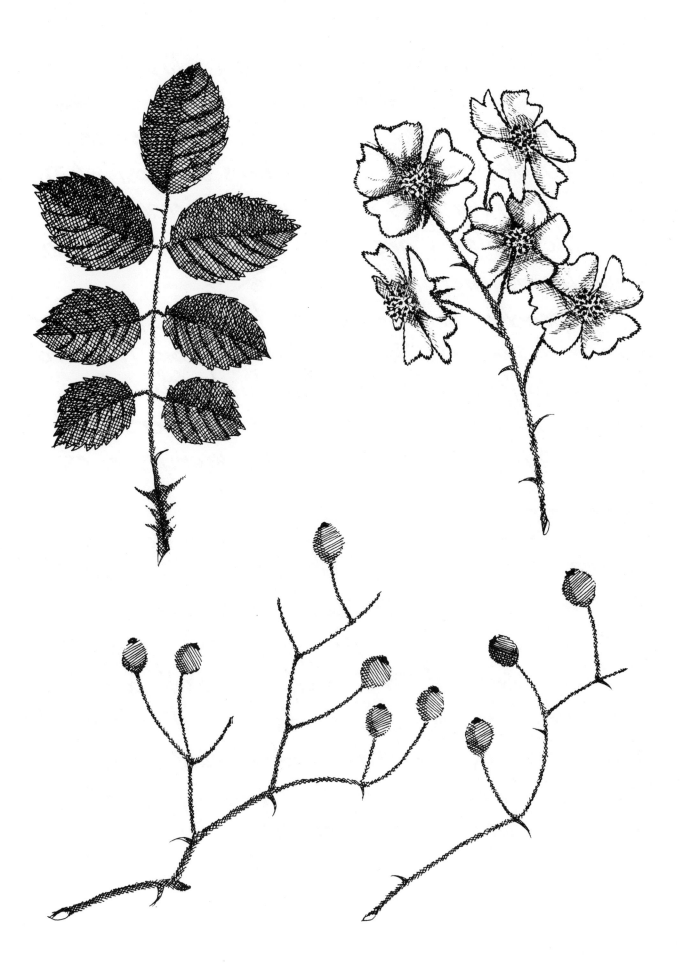

BLACKBERRIES probably attract more
species of birds than any other family of plants.
The family includes raspberries, dewberries,
and thimbleberries. The prickers on most of these
plants are numerous and sharp. Because of
this, these plants are best located in a corner
away from general activity.

Depending on the species, berries will be ripe
from mid-summer through fall. Among the birds
arriving to feed, watch for cardinals, thrushes,
sparrows, orioles, catbirds, and thrashers. A thick
stand also provides nesting sites for many species.

SUMACS are lovers of sunshine usually
growing in stands in upland fields. They form a
dense mass of green through the summer which
turns brilliant red in the fall. The berries are
in large clusters at the top of the plant, and by
mid-winter become an important food source. It
is a favorite of bluebirds, and I have seen as
many as twenty-one of these beautiful birds on
a small stand at one time.

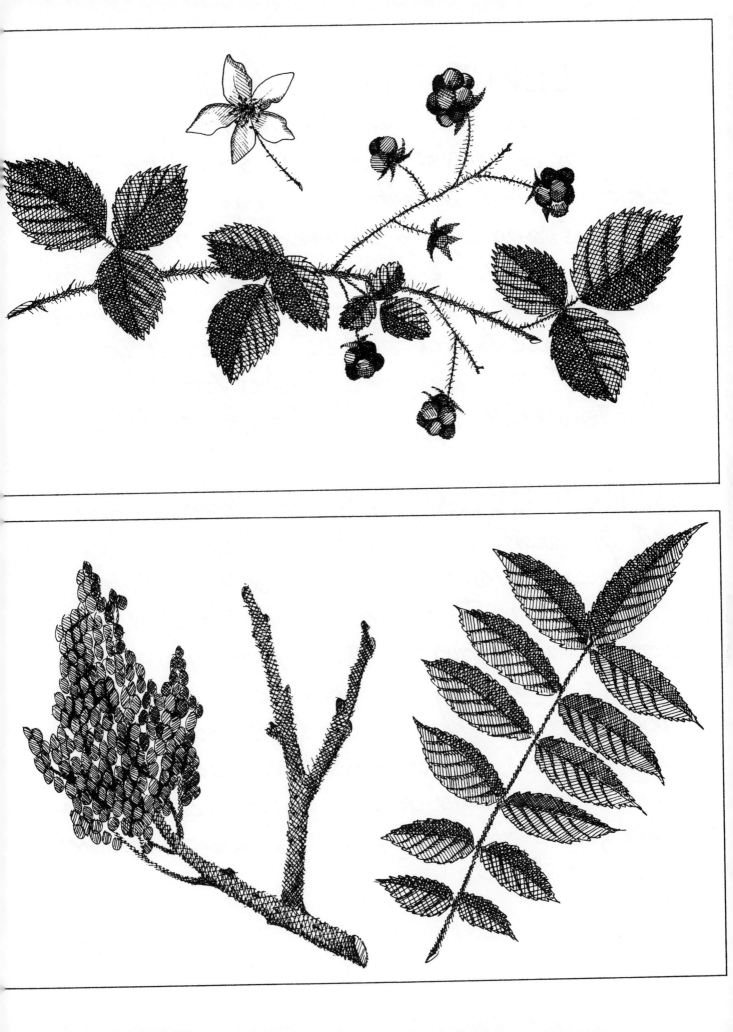

BLUEBERRY bushes are handsome plants.

They are densely branched, the new growth being red or reddish-green. In spring, pretty clusters of white bell-like flowers hang from the branches, and by mid-summer the berries are ripe. In fall, the blueberry bushes end the year with a brilliant display of red leaves. Even though you may love to pick and eat blueberries yourself, try to set aside a couple of bushes for the birds. It is remarkable how quickly the berries disappear!

SERVICEBERRIES are found through-out the country. They are called shadbushes or shadblow in New England because their April-May flowering time coincides with the shad migration up various rivers to their spawning grounds. Berries ripen early and become an important food source for thrushes, cardinals, mockingbirds, and catbirds. Serviceberries prefer somewhat moist ground, and do well in shade or sun. Their white flowers stand out among the bare branches of spring. ଚ୬ତ

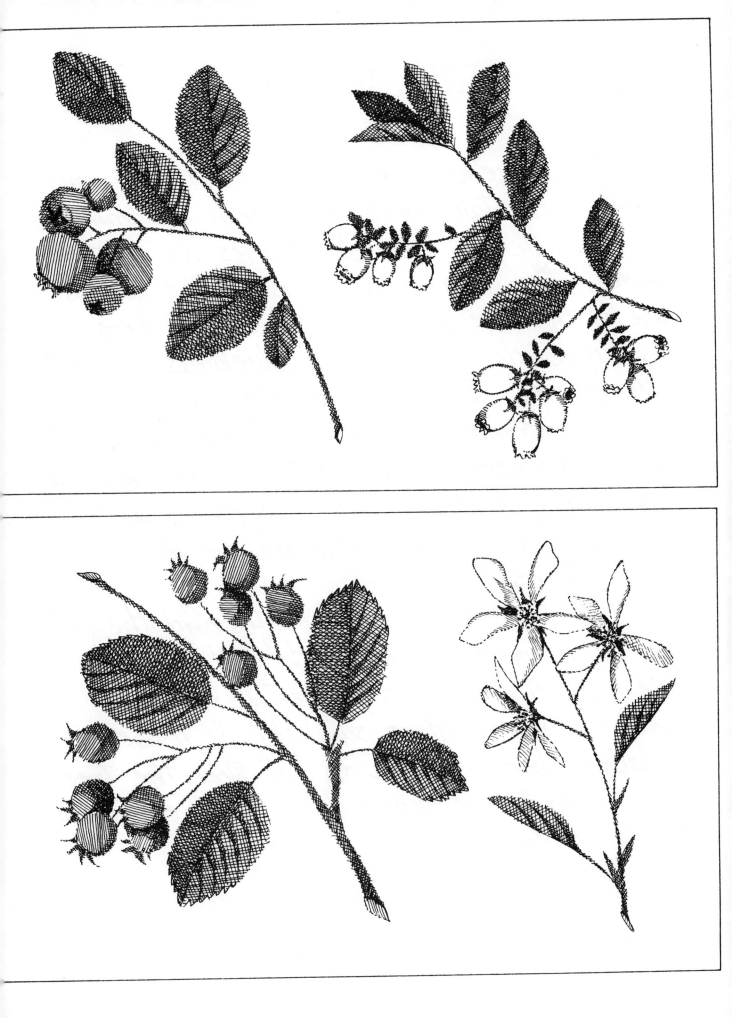

RED CEDAR

    Red cedar is a favorite plant with many birds. These tall conical evergreens are commonly found in fields. Their blue berries are relished; indeed, the cedar waxwing is named for its use of this tree as a food source. Flickers, mockingbirds, robins, and bluebirds also eat the berries. The prickly needles on the twigs and spring growth make a safe nesting site for many species. The nests of song, chipping, and field sparrows, as well as robins and brown thrashers can regularly be found in these trees.

    Its attractiveness to wildlife, and the fact that it is evergreen, make the red cedar an ideal plant for one's property. Its one major requirement is sunlight. If it becomes shaded, berry production will stop, the tree will begin to lose shape, and it will eventually die.

In addition to the plants already mentioned, the following are also very popular with birds:

Autumn Olive: a shrub introduced from Asia; clusters of red-orange berries; fast growing and bears fruit even while quite small.

Cherries: the many species include both trees and shrubs. Attracts thrushes, waxwings, and finches.

Hackberry: trees especially common in the midwest. Often used as ornamental plantings.

Grape: native species are eaten by over forty kinds of birds. Vines provide cover for nesting.

Elderberry: small shrub of moist areas which bears large flat clusters of purple berries.

Hawthorns: large berries on these short thorny trees are eaten by robins.

Mountain Ash: a tree of cool regions whose brilliant orange berries are quickly eaten by many species of birds.

Hollies: in eastern United States. Both evergreen and deciduous with bright red berries

HOUSE & FEEDER PLANS

Many of the house plans in this section are based on the design first set forth by Lewis Kibler for bluebird boxes. The measurements can be varied slightly in most cases and the effectiveness of the house or feeder will not change. Hole sizes are specific.

Most houses can be hung by putting 2 screwhooks (one above the other) in a post or tree, and drilling 2 small holes in the back of the box, so the box may just be hooked onto the post.

It is not difficult to construct your own feeders or bird houses. It is inexpensive and provides a great deal of satisfaction in watching the birds make use of your creations.

Materials must all be outdoor-hardy, so be sure to use woods that are weather resistant. Outdoor plywood works fine and it is modest in price. It is best to use $\frac{3}{4}$" for bird houses while $\frac{1}{2}$" will suffice for feeders. Make sure any nails or screws used are galvanized or of a rust resistant metal.

When it comes to painting, you may be as fancy as you wish. The important thing to remember is to use light colors, as dark colors absorb heat which could possibly kill the young. I put no paint on my houses, using only a wood stain on them to help protect the wood.

Houses + platforms must be cleaned out each year so that bird lice will not be present for next year's occupants. Houses should be set out by the end of March in the northern half of the country.

The Bluebird Box

TREE SWALLOWS TOO!

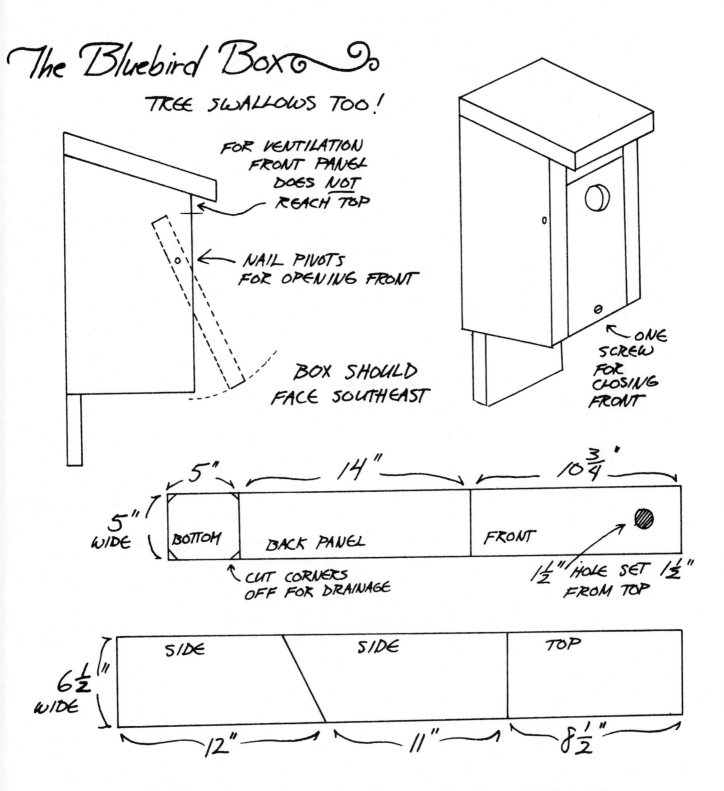

FOR VENTILATION FRONT PANEL DOES *NOT* REACH TOP

NAIL PIVOTS FOR OPENING FRONT

BOX SHOULD FACE SOUTHEAST

ONE SCREW FOR CLOSING FRONT

5"

14"

$10\frac{3}{4}$"

5" WIDE

BOTTOM

BACK PANEL

FRONT

CUT CORNERS OFF FOR DRAINAGE

$1\frac{1}{2}$" HOLE SET $1\frac{1}{2}$" FROM TOP

$6\frac{1}{2}$" WIDE

SIDE

SIDE

TOP

12"

11"

$8\frac{1}{2}$"

FOR BLUEBIRDS PLACE BOX ONLY 5 TO 6 FEET HIGH. FOR TREE SWALLOWS + THE WESTERN VIOLET-GREEN SWALLOW, HANG 6 TO 10 FEET UP. ALL 3 LIKE HOUSES IN THE OPEN, BLUEBIRDS NEAR FIELD EDGES + SWALLOWS NEAR WATER.

115

The House Wren Box

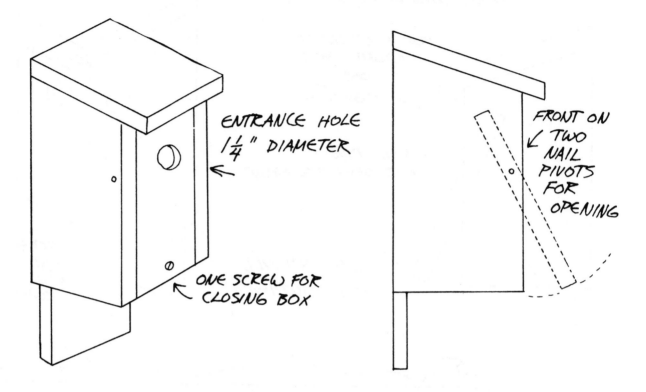

ENTRANCE HOLE 1¼" DIAMETER

ONE SCREW FOR CLOSING BOX

FRONT ON TWO NAIL PIVOTS FOR OPENING

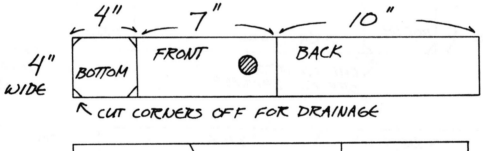

4" WIDE

4" ↔ BOTTOM | 7" ↔ FRONT | 10" ↔ BACK

↖ CUT CORNERS OFF FOR DRAINAGE

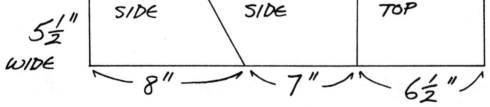

5½" WIDE

SIDE | SIDE | TOP

8" ↔ 7" ↔ 6½"

HOUSE WRENS ARE NOT PARTICULARLY CHOOSY ABOUT LOCATIONS, NESTING IN OPEN FIELDS, BUSHY AREAS, DECIDUOUS WOODLANDS, OR NEAR HOUSES. HEIGHT FROM THE GROUND CAN RANGE FROM 5 TO 10 FEET.

The Chickadee & Titmouse House

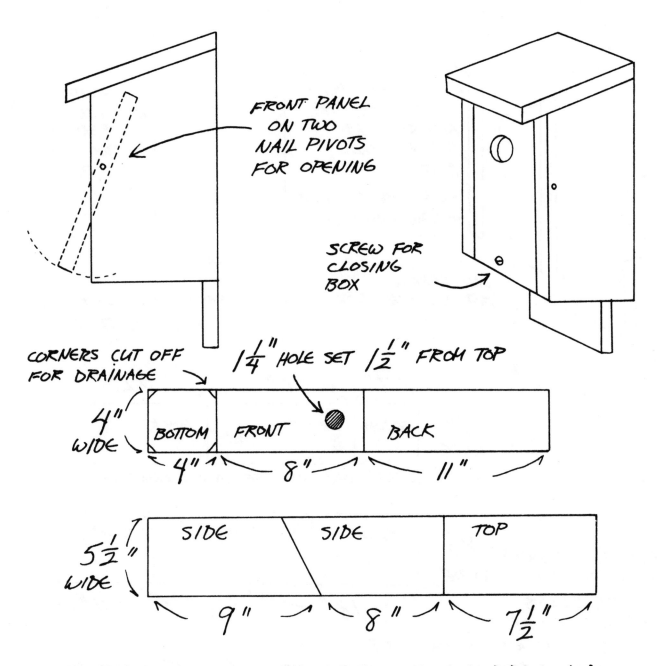

FRONT PANEL ON TWO NAIL PIVOTS FOR OPENING

SCREW FOR CLOSING BOX

CORNERS CUT OFF FOR DRAINAGE

$1\frac{1}{4}$" HOLE SET $1\frac{1}{2}$" FROM TOP

4" WIDE

BOTTOM	FRONT		BACK

4"   8"   11"

$5\frac{1}{2}$" WIDE

SIDE	SIDE	TOP

9"   8" $7\frac{1}{2}$"

CHICKADEES & TITMICE ARE BOTH WOODLAND BIRDS, AND AS SUCH PREFER TO USE BOXES PLACED ON TREES IN WOODS, 6 TO 12 FEET HIGH.

The Flicker, Kestrel, + Owl Box

ENTRANCE HOLE is 3" FOR THE KESTREL AND SCREECH OWL, BUT 2½" FOR THE FLICKER + SAW-WHET OWL

ONE SCREW FOR CLOSING BOX

FRONT PANEL SWINGS OPEN ON TWO NAIL PIVOTS

FACE BOX SOUTHEAST FOR KESTREL

7" WIDE

7"	16"	22"
BOTTOM	FRONT	BACK

CUT CORNERS OFF FOR DRAINAGE

FLICKERS + OWLS WILL OCCUPY THESE BOXES WHEN THEY ARE PLACED ON A TREE OR POST

8½" WIDE

SIDE	SIDE	TOP
18"	16"	11"

IN A WOODED AREA ANYWHERE FROM 6 TO 12 FEET ABOVE THE GROUND. SCREECH OWLS MAY ALSO BE FOUND USING THE WOOD DUCK NEST-BOX. KESTRELS PREFER TO BE IN THE OPEN OR ALONG A WOODED EDGE 10 OR MORE FEET UP.

The Wood Duck Box

leather hinge

Tack on slab of rough bark

wood shavings replaced each winter

4" deep

screw eye + hook

sheet metal raccoon guard

constructed from planks of 1" rough lumber

21"	24"	21"	9"

10"

| side | side | front | bottom |

cut corners off for drainage

hole is wider than high: 3"x4" + center is 6" from top

12"

| back | cover |

cone of sheet metal

raccoon guard

Erect before middle of March.
Must be at least 15' from ground.
If not directly at or in water,
ground area must be hospitable to
ducklings jumping down from box.
If placed on pole in water, box should
be 5' above flood level.

Purple martin houses are expensive to buy and difficult to build, so it is a good idea to make sure that martins are in your area before undertaking such a project. Martins are quite common in some parts of the United States yet scarce in other areas.

If martins are present, then choose a location in the open. If there is water nearby, so much the better. The house must be at least 15 feet high, and as it is large and heavy, a sturdy pole must be used; the pole should also be easy to take down, so that the house may be cleaned each year.

Martin houses should be painted white to reflect the sun's rays and reduce heat inside. The roof can be another color, perhaps green.

In the north, the houses should be up by early April, since a vanguard of males often arrives to find locations before the rest of the flock arrives a month or so later.

The Purple Martin House

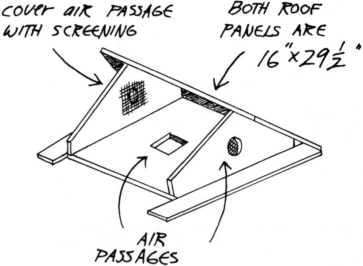

COVER AIR PASSAGE WITH SCREENING

BOTH ROOF PANELS ARE 16" x 29½"

ENTRANCE HOLES ARE 2½"

AIR PASSAGES

INSIDE PARTITIONS MAY BE ½" PLYWOOD

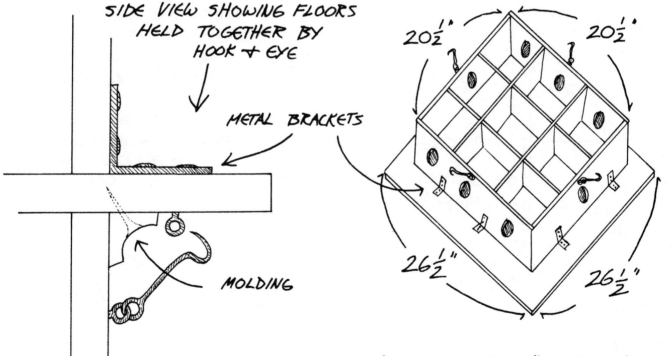

SIDE VIEW SHOWING FLOORS HELD TOGETHER BY HOOK + EYE

METAL BRACKETS

MOLDING

20½"

20½"

26½"

26½"

EACH "APARTMENT" IS 6" X 6" X 6"

The Robin, Phoebe, + Barn Swallow Nesting Platform

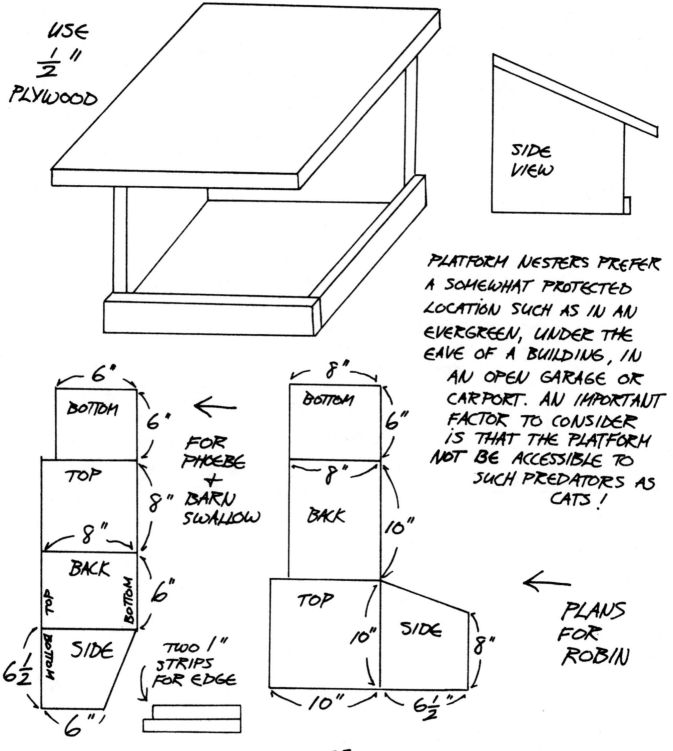

USE $\frac{1}{2}$" PLYWOOD

SIDE VIEW

PLATFORM NESTERS PREFER A SOMEWHAT PROTECTED LOCATION SUCH AS IN AN EVERGREEN, UNDER THE EAVE OF A BUILDING, IN AN OPEN GARAGE OR CARPORT. AN IMPORTANT FACTOR TO CONSIDER IS THAT THE PLATFORM NOT BE ACCESSIBLE TO SUCH PREDATORS AS CATS!

6"
BOTTOM
6"
TOP
8"
BACK
8"
6"
TOP
BOTTOM
SIDE
$6\frac{1}{2}$"
BOTTOM
6"

FOR PHOEBE + BARN SWALLOW

TWO 1" STRIPS FOR EDGE

8"
BOTTOM
6"
8"
BACK
10"
10"
TOP
SIDE
10"
8"
10"
$6\frac{1}{2}$"

PLANS FOR ROBIN

Simple Homemade Feeders

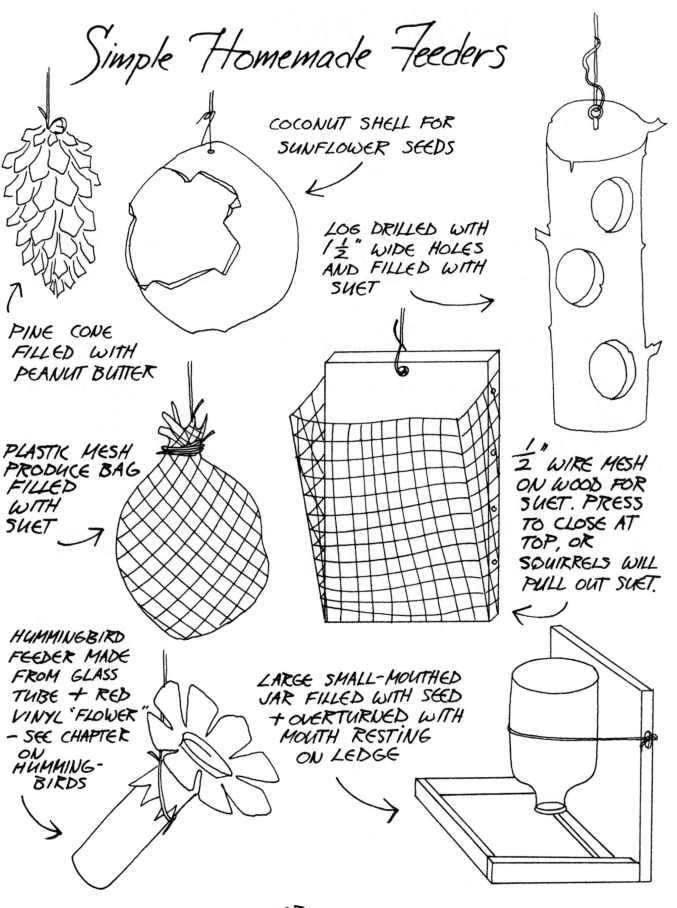

COCONUT SHELL FOR
SUNFLOWER SEEDS

LOG DRILLED WITH
$1\frac{1}{2}$" WIDE HOLES
AND FILLED WITH
SUET

PINE CONE
FILLED WITH
PEANUT BUTTER

PLASTIC MESH
PRODUCE BAG
FILLED
WITH
SUET

$\frac{1}{2}$" WIRE MESH
ON WOOD FOR
SUET. PRESS
TO CLOSE AT
TOP, OR
SQUIRRELS WILL
PULL OUT SUET.

HUMMINGBIRD
FEEDER MADE
FROM GLASS
TUBE + RED
VINYL "FLOWER"
- SEE CHAPTER
ON
HUMMING-
BIRDS

LARGE SMALL-MOUTHED
JAR FILLED WITH SEED
+ OVERTURNED WITH
MOUTH RESTING
ON LEDGE

123

BIBLIOGRAPHY

The following were used as references in the preparation of this book:

Bent, Arthur C.; _Life Histories of North American Birds_; Dover Publications Inc., New York. 1961-68.

Martin, Alexander C.; Herbert S. Zim, and Arnold Nelson; _American Wildlife + Plants: A Guide To Wildlife Food Habits_; Dover Publications Inc.; New York. 1951.

Terres, John K.; _Songbirds in Your Garden_; Thomas Y. Crowell, Co., New York. 1953.

124

ADDITIONAL REFERENCES

Field Guides:

Peterson, Roger T.; A Field Guide to the Birds;
Houghton Mifflin Co.; Boston. 1961.

Peterson, Roger T.; A Field Guide to Western
Birds; Houghton Mifflin Co.; Boston. 1961.

Robbins, Chandler, Bertel Bruun, + Herbert Zim;
Birds of North America; Golden Press; N.Y. 1966.

Books on Attracting Birds:

Arbib, Robert and Tony Soper; The Hungry
Bird Book; (revised edition) Ballantine Books;
New York. 1971.

Davison, Verne E.; Attracting Birds: From the
Prairies to the Atlantic. Thomas Y. Crowell
Co.; New York. 1967.

Dennis, John B.; A Complete Guide to Bird
Feeding; Knopf Publishers; New York. 1975.

McElroy, Thomas P.; New Handbook of Attracting
Birds; Knopf Publishers, N.Y. 1960.

WORDS BY THE ARTIST

Robert wrote the text, and I hand-
lettered it, and drew all the pictures. It wasn't
easy, but it _was_ exciting! The following is an
identification of my drawings by page number.
Page:

(Title page) - a barn swallow in flight.

9   Young bluebirds (eastern species).

17   House wren (and wren eggs on page 19.)

21   Black-capped chickadees.

23   Eastern tufted titmouse. This head was drawn
from a photograph (Robert's); the bird's crest is all
the way up because he is being held + banded —
an indignant bird, I'm sure.

27   Yellow-shafted flickers. Male left, female right.

28   Lower breast feather of flicker.

31   Male Kestrel. (Female - streaked front-page 32.)

33 + 35 Saw-whet owls.

36 + 37 Screech owls. The full-page view was drawn

from one of Robert's photos; and yes, owls often look a little cross-eyed when seen close-up!

41   Wood duck.

43   Purple martins. Female on right.

49   Barn swallow in flight. Again. Because I like him.

51   Adult robin. And a baby on page 53.

57   Eastern phoebe.

61 & 62   House finches. Male on 61. Female page 62.

63   Head of starling in summer.

65   Starling in winter plumage.

69   Male English sparrow.

75   At top: sunflower seeds, one unshelled; lower left, millet seed; lower right, thistle seed.

103   Flowering dogwood.

105   Multiflora rose.

107   Top: blackberry brambles; bottom - sumac.

109   Blueberry on top; serviceberry below.

111   Red cedar, with detail of spiny new growth.

128   Male kestrel in flight.

(I forgot page 89! - ruby-throated hummingbirds.)
The book is done. May it give you pleasure.

Monica